BIG BEND
OF THE
RIO GRANDE

PHOTOGRAPHS AND TEXT BY
LAURENCE PARENT

Sunset silhouettes the Chisos Mountains

Cover: Santa Elena Canyon

Inside front cover: Summer thunderstorms build over the Chisos Mountains

Page 1: The Sierra del Carmen rises above the Rio Grande

Laurence Parent would like to thank the people of Big Bend National Park, Far Flung Adventures, and the Texas Parks and Wildlife Department for their assistance, without which this book would never have been done.

Copyright 1993 by Big Bend Natural History Association
P. O. Box 68, Big Bend National Park, Texas 79834

ISBN 0-912001-19-4

Designed by Dwain Kelley
Austin, Texas

Pencil Illustrations by Don Collins

High on the pine-covered crest of the mountains of western Chihuahua, summer winds carry moisture up from the Pacific Ocean. As the air rises, it cools, and moisture condenses out, creating puffy, white cumulus clouds. With daytime heating, towering thunderheads billow into the sky. By late afternoon heavy rains fall on the Sierra Madre Occidental, the high mountain backbone of northern Mexico. The water cascades down the wooded slopes, creating rivulets and streams. The rushing mountain creeks merge to form the Rio Conchos. As the river flows out of the mountains, other tributaries join it. The Rio Conchos soon enters the Chihuahuan Desert for its long, dry crossing to the Rio Grande.

At the twin cities of Ojinaga, Mexico and Presidio, Texas, the Rio Conchos meets the Rio Grande at the international border. From its source high in the southern Rocky Mountains of Colorado, the Rio Grande winds its way 900 miles through three states and along the Texas-Mexico border before reaching the confluence at Presidio. Although the Rio Conchos contributes most of the flow to the combined river, it takes on the name of its smaller tributary and becomes the Rio Grande.

For 1000 miles the combined river forms the boundary between Mexico and the United States. In West Texas, the river funnels through a series of spectacular canyons in and adjoining Big Bend National Park. Downstream from Del Rio, the river passes through mesquite-studded land for hundreds of miles before finally reaching its flat, heavily cultivated delta at the Gulf of Mexico.

The river system drains one-quarter million square miles of land on its long voyage to the sea. For most of its length the river travels through arid desert. Its vital waters have attracted humans for at least 10,000 years. The Spanish explorer Piñeda sailed up the mouth of the river in 1519, naming it the Rio de las Palmas because of the thousands of acres of subtropical palms that forested the delta. Its American name means Great River, an ambiguous name in Mexico, because all major drainages are known as Great Rivers. The Mexicans call it Rio Bravo, or Wild River, a name given by Don Juan de Oñate's scouts in 1598 after some of their horses drowned during spring floods near El Paso.

Before European settlement of the Southwest, the Rio Grande deserved the name Great River. The river that was called "a mile wide, a foot deep, too thin to plow and too thick to drink, always flooding, and always changing beds" has been controlled and harnessed within the last three hundred years. Within a few miles of its source in Colorado, the Rio Grande encounters its first dam. Many more dams, large and small, control and allocate the river's flow as it passes through Colorado, New Mexico, and the El Paso-Juarez valley. Along the way it irrigates several hundred thousand acres of cropland. With no major tributaries between the Chama River in northern New Mexico and the Rio Conchos in the Big Bend, the river shrinks steadily from evaporation and the intensive use of its waters.

By the time the Rio Grande flows past Fort Hancock and McNary below El Paso, it has dwindled to a trickle. The remnant waters enter a long narrow desert valley below the Quitman Mountains and disappear into the desert sands. Often the riverbed is dry for the next 100-plus miles. Then, in the heart of the desolate Chihuahuan Desert, the Rio Grande joins the much larger flow of Mexico's Rio Conchos.

Although the Rio Conchos has been dammed in Mexico, it still retains a much larger portion of its original flow than does the upper Rio Grande. The Rio Conchos is less utilized for agricultural and urban purposes, plus it does not flow through as many miles of dry country as the upper Rio Grande. However, massive logging projects are planned high in its watershed in the Sierra Madre. Large-scale deforestation is expected to cause flooding, erosion, and higher rates of flow during rainy periods and lower water levels during dry times. Additionally, the road system built for the

Cenizo

Hiker in the Chisos Mountains

Pines and other conifers blanket the mountain headwaters of the Rio Conchos and Rio Grande

logging operations will likely encourage other development and increase water consumption.

For more than 1000 miles, from El Paso downstream to the Gulf of Mexico, the Rio Grande forms the boundary between Texas and Mexico. Before the Republic of Texas won its independence in 1836, the river was part of Mexico. After the war for independence, Texas claimed the Rio Grande as its boundary with Mexico, rather than the Nueces River, claimed by the Mexicans. After Texas was annexed into the United States in 1845, the boundary dispute helped lead to the Mexican-American War of 1846. With Mexico's defeat, Santa Ana signed the Treaty of Guadalupe Hidalgo in 1848 ceding the lands north of the Rio Grande to the United States.

Although the Rio Grande forms a political boundary between two nations, the river creates many ties between residents along both sides of the border. The river valley attracted Mexican and American settlers because ample water allowed farming in the dry desert. Many families have members on both sides of the river, and residents speak Spanish and English, or some mix thereof, on both sides of the river. Trade between the two countries centers in cities lining the river banks.

Nature does not recognize political boundaries. For much of the river's passage along the Texas-Mexico border, the Chihuahuan Desert dominates the landscape. Spiny lechuguilla and sotol plants dot the hillsides in both countries. Colorful cacti bloom in the spring, brightening the desert with splashes of red and yellow. Deer and javelina roam the river bottom. High above, red-tailed hawks circle patiently, drifting indiscriminately across the border. Black bears and mountain lions cross the river into Big Bend National Park from the Sierra del Carmen of Mexico in search of new territory. The landscape is least disturbed by human activity along the river as it flows through the Big Bend country of West Texas and northern Mexico.

Bobcat

US 67

Glass Mountains

385

Del Norte Mountains

Marathon

2400

285

U.S. 90

349

Sanderson

Dryden

Woods Hollow Mountains

Pecos River

90

Santiago Mountains

Langtry

385

Rio Grande

2627

BLACK GAP
WILDLIFE
MANAGEMENT
AREA

THE LOWER CANYONS

Rosillos
Mountains

Dead Horse Mountains

Lake Amistad

Christmas
Mountains

La Linda

Park
Headquarters

Butte

Basin

Rio Grande
Village

BOQUILLAS
CANYON

Chisos Mountains

Castolon

BIG BEND
NATIONAL PARK

Boquillas
del Carmen

Sierra del Carmen

Mariscal
Mountain

San
Vicente

MARISCAL
CANYON

SWAIN KELLEY

BIG BEND
OF THE
RIO GRANDE

THE RIO GRANDE IN THE BIG BEND COUNTRY

One of the most spectacular sections of the Rio Grande and its tributaries lies between Presidio and Langtry. There, the river has carved a series of sheer-walled canyons, some over 1500 feet deep, as it makes its great curve, or bend, changing flow direction from southeast to northeast. Although the rugged desert area is lightly settled, it has become famous as the site of several parks, including Big Bend National Park, Big Bend Ranch State Natural Area, Black Gap Wildlife Management Area, the Rio Grande Wild and Scenic River, and a proposed protected area in Mexico. The parks limit development in the Big Bend country.

Long before the canyons formed, ancient seas covered much of the Big Bend. The land rose and fell, lifting the sea beds into mountains and then eroding them away. During the Cretaceous Period about 200 million years ago, massive beds of limestone developed from the accumulating calcium carbonate shells of ocean creatures.

Author Kerri Nelson discusses two theories about the formation of the canyons in her book, *The Roadside Geology of Big Bend National Park*. About 75-100 million years ago the thick beds of limestone were faulted, folded, and uplifted into mountains. In the antecedent theory, the mountains rose and the pre-existing Rio Conchos was forced to cut down into the bedrock in its voyage to the sea. The thick, durable limestone layers formed sheer walled canyons as the river cut deeper and deeper. Eventually Santa Elena, Mariscal,

and Boquillas canyons of Big Bend National Park and the Lower Canyons of the Rio Grande Wild and Scenic River were created.

In the superimposed theory, the ancestral Rio Grande flowed across the coastal plain east of the Sierra del Carmen. To the west, folding and faulting formed basins with no drainage. Sediment eroded from the uplifted fault blocks and the Chisos Mountains washed into the basins. As each basin filled, it overflowed into the next lower basin, eventually forming one large connected basin in northern Mexico. Finally, as the mountains rose and precipitation increased, the basin overflowed, breaching the Sierra del Carmen and connecting with the Rio Grande on the coastal plain.

Colorado Canyon, upstream from

An agave thrives below Casa Grande Peak in the Chisos Mountains

Rain falls over the Rio Grande and distant Chisos Mountains

Strawberry cactus

Aspens in the Chisos Mountains receive more rain than the desert below

Lajitas in Big Bend Ranch State Natural Area, formed as the river carved a path through the much newer lavas of the Sierra Rica and Bofecillos volcanoes.

The Rio Grande upstream of the confluence with the Rio Conchos did not join with the flow of the Conchos until much later, possibly as recently as 500,000 years ago. Thus the complete Rio Grande, from Colorado to the Gulf of Mexico, is a very young river.

The Rio Grande in the Big Bend area lies entirely within the Chihuahuan Desert. The Chihuahuan Desert is one of the four great North American deserts; the Sonoran, the Mojave, and the Great Basin deserts lie to the north and west. The Chihuahuan Desert covers much of northern Mexico and spills over into West Texas and part of southern New Mexico. Big Bend National Park protects America's best example of Chihuahuan Desert. As with all deserts, it is characterized by average rainfall of less than ten inches annually at lower elevations.

The Chihuahuan Desert's plant life sets it apart from other deserts. One plant in particular, the lechuguilla, is called an indicator plant for the Chihuahuan Desert; it is an endemic plant to that area. Its leaves grow in a green rosette of thick fibrous blades tipped with needle-sharp spines. The plants can grow into thick patches that are difficult to cross without spearing an ankle.

A lechuguilla blooms only once in its life. After building up a food supply for as much as ten or fifteen years, it quickly sends up a green asparagus-like stalk ten or more feet tall. After the stalk flowers, the entire plant dies, its food supply exhausted.

The sharp spines protect the lechuguilla from many enemies, but several animals still manage to eat it. The javelina often digs up the plant to eat the heart, roots, and soft parts at the base of the blades. The pocket gopher avoids the spines altogether by eating out the heart of the plant from underground tunnels. Deer often eat the tender, unprotected flowering stalks before they bloom.

The sotol, another plant common in the Chihuahuan Desert, thrives on desert slopes in the foothills of the Chisos Mountains. Its long narrow leaves radiate outward from the plant's center. The bright green leaves are lined with rows of small hook-like spines and resemble a saw blade.

The ocotillo usually appears to be nothing but a ragged bundle of dead sticks reaching ten or fifteen feet into the air. After a soaking rain, however, the plant quickly takes advantage of the moisture by sprouting small green leaves all along the seemingly dead stalks. In spring, bright red tassels of flowers adorn the ends of the branches. As with many desert plants, rows of sharp spines line the woody branches.

Numerous species of cacti thrive in the Chihuahuan Desert. To survive in hot, arid conditions, cacti have developed thick, waxy skins to slow transpiration of water. To reduce evaporative surface area, the plants have no leaves and produce their food with chlorophyll in the skin. Spines of many shapes and sizes, from delicate fishhooks to thick, straight needles, armor cacti. The spines protect the plant's moist body from foraging animals and shade its surface from the sun.

The creosote bush is one of the most common plants along the Rio Grande. The evergreen shrub usually grows three or four feet tall and has small, waxy, green leaves. The plant not only uses an extensive system of shallow surface roots to capture moisture from brief rain showers, but a taproot reaching as much as thirty feet into the ground. Because few animals will eat creosote bush, it

Javelina

tends to spread and multiply when overgrazing lessens its competition. After rainstorms, it perfumes the desert with a fresh, astringent fragrance.

Candelilla, or wax plant, thrives on hot limestone ledges above the river. It grows in thick clumps of blue-green pencil-size stalks. To help limit moisture loss, it produces a high grade wax coating on its skin. Mexican citizens harvest the plant to extract the wax for a multitude of uses, including wood finishes, candles, and food products.

The river creates a ribbon of green, a riparian area, which contrasts starkly with the surrounding desert. The sandy floodplain of the river supports plants that need more moisture than the modest desert rains provide. Grasses, in particular the non-native Bermuda grass, carpet the river banks. Two types of large grasses, the common and giant reed, grow up to fifteen feet tall in dense, almost impassible thickets. The reed provides food and shelter to many animals, from the wood rat and Trans-Pecos copperhead to the beaver and mule deer.

Willows and cottonwoods send their roots deep into the sandy floodplain soil,

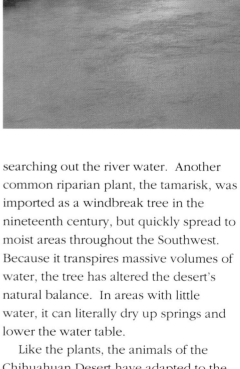

The waters of the Rio Grande create a lush riparian corridor through the desert

White-winged dove

searching out the river water. Another common riparian plant, the tamarisk, was imported as a windbreak tree in the nineteenth century, but quickly spread to moist areas throughout the Southwest. Because it transpires massive volumes of water, the tree has altered the desert's natural balance. In areas with little water, it can literally dry up springs and lower the water table.

Like the plants, the animals of the Chihuahuan Desert have adapted to the hot arid climate. In the heat of a summer day, the desert may seem

12

Mountain lion

lifeless, except for the whine of cicadas and a few vultures circling high overhead. To avoid the heat and excessive water loss, many creatures are nocturnal.

At night, the desert comes alive. Insects crawl out from underneath rocks and ledges. Rodents scurry out of their burrows to nibble on green plants and seeds. Desert cottontails leave their hiding places in search of food. Mule deer rise from shady beds tucked under trees and shrubs. The predators also emerge in the coolness of dusk to search for prey. Snakes pursue rats and mice, guided by smell or their prey's body heat. The owl, aided by superb night vision, drifts above the desert floor, searching for rabbits, rodents, and other small creatures. The mountain lion silently stalks its primary quarry, the mule deer. Bats flit through the night sky, locating flying insects with reflected sound waves, or sonar. At dawn, the guard changes: nocturnal creatures retreat from the heat, while many birds greet the sun with a chorus of calls.

Although many different animals

regularly visit the Rio Grande for water, several center their lives in the narrow green river corridor. Three species of catfish scavenge along the river bottom, well hidden in the muddy water. At dusk, observers at the river may hear a splash, see a ripple of movement, or find the gnawed trunks of willows and cottonwoods on the bank. The bank beaver thrives in the perennially flowing river, feeding on the bark of trees growing on the floodplain. Unlike beavers in other parts of the United States, those at Big Bend live in burrows in the river banks rather than in wood and mud lodges. Before overgrazing and ground water pumping dried up many Rio Grande tributaries such as Terlingua and Tornillo Creeks, beavers were much more common in the Big Bend area. The book *Big Bend*, by the National Park Service, relates that James Gillett, foreman of the G-4 ranch, found in 1885 that "the Terlingua was a bold running stream, studded with cottonwood timber and alive with beaver."

The endangered peregrine falcon favors the sheer cliffs of the river canyons for its aerie. Eggs and young are safe from predators when perched high on inaccessible ledges. Birds, attracted to the greenery and permanent water of the river corridor, provide abundant prey. The peregrine dives, or "stoops," on its victims from great heights at speeds in excess of 150 miles per hour. Because of the bird's endangered status, the National Park Service makes a special effort to protect the falcons during the breeding season.

Peregrine falcons favor the high cliffs of river canyons, such as Boquillas, for their aeries

Cottonwoods and beaver are rare today along Terlingua Creek

PEOPLE COME TO THE BIG BEND COUNTRY

Humans are relative latecomers to the Rio Grande in the Big Bend area, but have inhabited the area for at least ten thousand years. The earliest people were probably hunters following herds of now-extinct bison, horses, mammoths, and other animals in the cool, lush period of the last ice age. As the climate warmed and dried at the end of the glacial period, these early people either adapted to the changing climate, moved on, or died out. Very little is known of these early inhabitants.

Later, the area along the Rio Grande was used by groups of hunter-gatherers adapted to desert life. They moved constantly, living in caves and shelters near the river and other water sources. They hunted desert animals and gathered prickly pear fruits, pinyon nuts, mesquite beans, agave and sotol hearts, and many other edibles. From the fibrous leaves of yucca, lechuguilla, and basketgrass, they wove baskets and sandals. Archaeologists still find remnants of their handiwork preserved in dry desert caves.

Although the archaeological record is not clear, evidently the hunter-gatherers were eventually displaced or absorbed into other groups. The Patarabueye later settled the river valley at the confluence of the Rio Grande and the Rio Conchos, establishing villages and farms along the fertile river bottom. They were influenced by the prosperous pueblo culture that lay upstream along the Rio Grande in what is now New Mexico. By the time the Spaniards arrived, it appears that a nomadic group sometimes known as the Jumanos had settled at least seasonally with the Patarabueye.

Although Cabeza de Vaca's account is not clear, he may have been the first European to encounter the Patarabueye and Jumanos in 1535. After Coronado's expedition of 1540 failed to find gold and riches in New Mexico and Arizona, the Southwest, including the Big Bend region of Texas, was largely ignored for many years. The Big Bend area came to be known as *el despoblado*, or the uninhabited land. The first documented

Indian grinding holes line the floor of a rock shelter at Big Bend Ranch State Natural Area

contact with the people at the river confluence, called La Junta by the Spaniards, came during the expedition of Fray Agustín Rodríguez in 1581.

Scattered expeditions crossed the Big Bend country during following years, but, for the most part, the Spanish avoided *el despoblado.* The land was harsh and difficult to cross, with few riches to be found. Attempts to enslave Indians to sell to mine owners led to hostilities. A missionary effort was initiated as early as 1684 at La Junta, but it was abandoned under pressure from

Indian raids.

By the late seventeenth century, Mescalero Apaches began moving south to the Big Bend country, themselves pushed from the north by Comanches and Utes. The Apaches rarely established permanent camps in the Big Bend. With their ability to live off the land, they could travel light and easily plunder the Spanish settlements of northern Mexico. To combat the raids, the Spaniards created a line of defensive forts to protect their northern frontier along the Rio Grande. The forts, or

Little more than adobe ruins remain of farms that once lined the river near Castolon

17

presidios, were established at La Junta in 1760, and at San Vicente, on the Mexican side of the river upstream from Rio Grande Village, and at San Carlos, south of Lajitas, in about 1773.

Although the Spaniards attempted to defeat the Apaches, the isolated presidios and small contingents of poorly equipped troops were ineffective. The forts at San Carlos and San Vicente were soon abandoned and Spain's northern frontier in the New World slipped south of the Rio Grande. Soon, however, the Comanches, bitter enemies of both the Apaches and Spaniards, began passing through the Big Bend country. Every year for more than 100 years, the Comanches raided deep into Mexico during the full moon of September. The appearance every autumn of the Comanche moon struck fear into the hearts of the Indian and Spanish inhabitants of Mexico as far south as Durango. The raiders crossed into today's Big Bend National Park through

Persimmon Gap and forded the river at Lajitas on their annual forays. On their return, they carried captured livestock, people, and loot back across the river.

Sharing the common threat of the Comanches, the Spaniards and Apaches became allies at the end of the eighteenth century and relative peace ensued along the Rio Grande. However, the Spanish government lost its territorial claims with Mexico's successful bid for independence in 1821. With the Spaniards gone, the Comanche raids commenced again, creating more of a threat to Mexico's frontier than had the Apache Indians. The Comanche and Apache again ruled the Big Bend country.

It was not until the 1870s that the Comanches were finally defeated by American troops in Oklahoma and the High Plains of Texas. For years after their defeat, the great Comanche trail was an obvious bare scar and trail of

Indian petroglyphs

bones across the Big Bend desert.

Few Americans ventured into the Big Bend country until after the Mexican-American War ended in 1848 and the border between Mexico and the United States was firmly established. Sporadic efforts to establish a trade route between New Orleans and the Mexican city of Chihuahua met with only limited success. In 1848, Ben Leaton built a fort and trading post near La Junta, the present site of Presidio, Texas and Ojinaga, Mexico. Now preserved at Fort Leaton State Historical Park, his fort was the first American settlement in the Big Bend region.

In the 1850s, several efforts were made to explore and map the Rio Grande through the Big Bend country. Efforts to navigate the river met with disaster in the rugged canyons. The Chandler-Green expedition managed to survey most of the river, enduring brutal overland climbs above Colorado, Santa Elena, Mariscal, and Boquillas canyons in 1852. The Michler survey party completed the survey through the Lower Canyons to the confluence with the Pecos River a year later by bypassing some canyons and floating others. The difficulty of the survey convinced the explorers that the river would never serve as a navigable waterway through the Big Bend region.

In 1880, Victorio's band of Apaches was defeated in the Mexican state of Chihuahua and the threat of Indian attack ended. In 1882, the first railroad crossed West Texas. The last wild stretch of the Rio Grande was open for settlement and exploitation.

Ranchers accelerated their movement into the apparently rich desert grasslands along the Rio Grande. As more and more ranchers moved into the area, the

open range soon disappeared, with fences closing the last in the early 1900s.

Miners and prospectors scoured the hills for riches on both sides of the Rio Grande. Silver was found north of the twin towns of Presidio and Ojinaga in the Chinati Mountains. The town of Shafter quickly grew to support the mines. Over twenty million dollars of silver was removed before the ore ran out early this century. Today, adobe ruins slowly disintegrate under the assault of desert thunderstorms. Only a few people reside in the former boomtown.

Mercury mines sparked the growth of Terlingua at the turn of the century

19

Abandoned Mariscal mercury mine

A rainbow cactus blooms on Mariscal Mountain

Lead, zinc, and silver ore was discovered in the Sierra del Carmen above the Mexican village of Boquillas. To transport the ore, a six-mile aerial tramway was built across the Rio Grande to a terminal on the Texas side. From there, the ore was hauled by wagon and truck to the railroad in Marathon. While the tramway was in operation from 1909 to 1919, ore buckets carried seven and one-half tons per hour. Now only rusting cables and collapsed wooden towers lie in the desert north of the river, across from Boquillas.

Cinnabar proved to be the most important mineral found along the Rio Grande. For years, rumors of quicksilver circulated in the Big Bend country. Mining began in earnest in the hills around Terlingua in 1894. The district soon became the second largest producer of mercury in the United States, producing 150,000 flasks of mercury by the time the last mine closed in 1941. A smaller mine operated at Mariscal Mountain a few miles north of Mariscal Canyon in what is now Big Bend

National Park. Unlike the mines in Terlingua, it never produced large quantities of quicksilver. Today, the mine workings have crumbled into ruins, and a much smaller Terlingua is dependent on visitors floating the Rio Grande and touring the state and national parks.

The mining did lasting damage to the land along the river. Cottonwoods and willows were clear-cut to fire the smelters and provide mine timbers and firewood. Farms were established in the Rio Grande's floodplain at Castolon, Rio Grande Village, and along Terlingua Creek at Terlingua Abaja to feed the miners. Some were overworked, leaving the soil depleted and open to invader species when the fields were abandoned. Cattle, goats, and sheep from area ranches overgrazed the desert grasslands.

Although the threat of Indian attack had ended by the late nineteenth century, the Rio Grande was not always peaceful. Both Mexican and American bandits used the lightly populated region as a hideout after committing crimes. With little law enforcement, the lawbreakers could flee across the river to escape from American or Mexican authorities. The Big Bend "is a favorable resort of the murderers and desperadoes driven from other sections of the state," claimed local citizens who requested more protection in a story in the August 9, 1879 *San Antonio Daily Express*.

The Mexican Revolution in 1911 caused increased violence along the river. Mexican revolutionaries crossed the river into the United States, fleeing Mexican troops or seeking recruits to their cause. Refugees fled to Marfa and other West Texas towns after Pancho Villa's forces attacked Ojinaga, across the river from Presidio. Frequent raids and battles across the border frightened Texas residents. Boquillas and San Vicente, just across the river from today's Big Bend National Park, were raided by bandits in 1912. Surprisingly, most of the few U.S. troops still in the Big Bend were withdrawn early in 1913. Soon the bandits raided ranches on the American side of the river, some as far north as Alpine. Laden with plundered guns, livestock, and provisions, the raiders would escape back across the river with little opposition. Some of the raids carried out by Villa's men may have been in retaliation for President Woodrow Wilson's discontinuation of financial aid to Villa. Many others were carried out by opportunistic gangs of bandits.

On the night of May 5, 1916, approximately eighty bandits crossed the river at San Vicente and raided the settlements of Glenn Springs and Boquillas, killing several residents, looting the villages, and taking prisoners back into Mexico. Major George Langhorne led troops across the border in pursuit of the bandits and ultimately recovered much of the stolen property

and killed, captured, or dispersed most of the raiders. The captives escaped or were released by the bandits.

After the raid, National Guardsmen were stationed along the border, quelling the unrest for a time. Soon, however, many of the troops were transferred to the war in Europe, and raiders again crossed the river from Mexico. Several small raids occurred over the next few years, but as the Mexican political situation stabilized, lasting peace finally came to the Rio Grande.

As early as 1916, government troops stationed at Big Bend proposed that the rugged country along the Rio Grande be made into a national park. However, it wasn't until state congressman R. M. Wagstaff of Abilene pushed through legislation in Austin in 1933 that a new park called Texas Canyons State Park and then Big Bend State Park was established. In 1935, President Franklin

Dawn in Mariscal Canyon

21

Roosevelt signed federal legislation establishing Big Bend National Park contingent upon acquisition of land by the state of Texas. Over the following years, the land was slowly acquired and was deeded to the federal government in 1944.

In more recent years, the spectacular country along adjoining sections of the Rio Grande has attracted additional protection. The Texas Parks and Wildlife Department administers the large Black Gap Wildlife Management Area downstream from the park, bordering part of the Lower Canyons of the Rio Grande. In 1978, Congress designated 191 miles of the Rio Grande from west of Mariscal Canyon through the Lower Canyons to just west of Langtry as a national wild and scenic river. Most recently, in 1988, the Texas Parks and Wildlife Department created the huge 250,000-acre Big Bend Ranch State Natural Area along Colorado Canyon, upstream from Lajitas. Now, the spectacular West Texas canyons of the Rio Grande all have some form of legal protection on the American side.

In Mexico, attempts were made as early as 1935 to create a sister park to Big Bend National Park. After several failures, Mexican officials have recently shown renewed interest in creating a protected area centered around the Sierra del Carmen, south of Boquillas Canyon. Someday the Rio Grande may pass through a huge international park as it flows through the rugged Big Bend country of Texas and Mexico.

The spindly ocotillo and other plants thrive in Colorado Canyon

The Rio Grande forms the southern boundary of Big Bend Ranch State Natural Area

THE CANYONS

COLORADO CANYON

At the twin cities of Presidio and Ojinaga, the Rio Conchos revitalizes the often dry and lifeless Rio Grande with waters originating in the extensive Sierra Madre of northwestern Mexico. Farmers still cultivate the broad valley today, as did the Patarabueye hundreds of years before them.

A highway, Texas FM 170, follows the river from Presidio to Lajitas, giving easy access to Colorado Canyon, the first major canyon of the Big Bend. The steep, windy drive is one of the most scenic in Texas.

Just downstream from Presidio, Fort Leaton State Historical Park bakes in the sun above the river bank on the Texas side. The old adobe fort has been well preserved by the dry desert climate. The

Closed Canyon forms a narrow slot at Big Bend Ranch

A blind prickly pear clings to the rim of Colorado Canyon

23

Texas Parks and Wildlife Department now manages the fort as a museum and historic site.

After Fort Leaton, the broad gravel wash of Alamito Creek joins the Rio Grande on the Texas side. Although the creek usually contains only a small water flow where it meets the river, its watershed includes a large area of Presidio County, extending as far north as Marfa. From Alamito Creek the river slowly winds its way southeast, meandering past fields and small villages. At Redford, Texas, farms cover a particularly broad swath of floodplain. Below Redford and the Mexican village of El Mulato, named for black Buffalo soldiers who settled there, the river valley narrows, eventually squeezing out the last of the farms. The mountains creep closer and closer to the river, and the valley becomes Colorado Canyon. A Spanish word for red or colorful, *colorado,* gives the red-walled canyon its name.

Downstream from Lajitas, the Rio Grande has cut its canyons through massive beds of sedimentary rock, mostly limestone of the Cretaceous Period. However, unlike those canyons, the river carved its way through thick layers of igneous rocks between Redford and Lajitas. The rusty, brownish-red canyon walls rise higher and higher as the Bofecillos Mountains of Texas and the Sierra Rica of Mexico crowd close to the river. The mountains, formed by volcanoes that erupted about 25 to 40 million years ago during the Tertiary Period, are much younger than the limestone beds.

The Rio Grande meanders through a broad farming valley near Redford

Volcanoes on both sides of the river erupted many times, spewing vast quantities of lava and ash across the land. The lava solidified into basalt, the hard, erosion-resistant rock that forms the sheer walls of the canyon. The deposits of soft, whitish rock in the canyon resulted from great explosions of hot, glowing ash that rained down in thick layers onto the ground. Heat and compression from succeeding layers hardened the ash beds into a soft rock called tuff. Weather has eroded the tuff into fanciful pinnacles in several places along the river.

The moon rises over eroded volcanic tuff

The 400-square-mile Big Bend Ranch State Natural Area first touches the river a few miles upstream from Redford, but does not front the river relatively continuously until about halfway to Lajitas. Several sheer-walled side canyons, including Tapado, Rancherías, Panther, Madera, and Fresno, tumble out of the craggy heights of the Bofecillos Mountains, cross FM 170, and intersect the river. Except during and after heavy rains, the side canyons are usually dry. Fresno Canyon, with the biggest drainage area and several springs in its headwaters, is the most likely to have water. A marked hiking trail follows Rancherías Canyon from the highway into the heart of the rugged Bofecillos Mountains.

The most popular put-in for boaters in Colorado Canyon lies on the small floodplain where Rancherías Canyon joins the river. Below the put-in, the river enters sheer-walled Colorado Canyon. The most spectacular part of the canyon lies under what locals call the Big Hill on FM 170 and Mesa Santana on the Mexican side. The canyon wall on the Texas riverbank rises 500 feet in a sheer cliff. From the highway on top, the cliff makes a vertigo-inducing plunge straight into the river. To the east, the view stretches from Colorado Canyon to the steel-blue, monochrome outline of the distant Chisos Mountains.

For the most part, the Rio Grande flows from Presidio to Lajitas with little more than ripples breaking its smooth, glassy surface. However, once the river enters Colorado Canyon, several rapids break the calm and liven up the river. The accumulated inflow of boulders and debris from large tributaries cause most of the rapids. Panther Creek's deposits create the largest rapid in the canyon. Ledgerock Rapid can also be exciting, but neither should present a problem if scouted first and run by an experienced boater.

After the Big Hill, the canyon walls recede as the river flows out of the heart of the Bofecillos Mountains and Sierra Rica, and finally disappear altogether at Lajitas. Lajitas, a small town on the Texas side of the Rio Grande matched by a village of the same name across the river in Mexico, lies at one of the river's historical crossing points. The rugged Bofecillos Mountains and Sierra Rica to the west and the high Mesa de Anguila to the east funnel traffic into the low valley at Lajitas. Prehistoric people undoubtedly used the crossing when going north or south. The river crossing

is probably most famous as the western fork of the route used by the Comanches on their annual fall raids into northern Mexico. Many others, from government troops and bandits early this century to tourists today, have used the crossing to avoid the rugged terrain both upstream and downstream along the Rio Grande.

Small as it is, Lajitas is the largest settlement on the American side of the river between Redford and Langtry, which lies 260 miles downstream. The Lajitas Trading Post still serves local residents on both sides of the river, as it has since the early 1900s. The town now thrives as a tourist center for river boaters and other people visiting the Big Bend country. Visitors wanting to float Colorado Canyon or visit Big Bend Ranch State Natural Area should stop at park headquarters at the Barton Warnock Environmental Education Center on the east side of town to get permits and information.

Yellow rocknettle brightens cliffs in Colorado Canyon

SANTA ELENA CANYON

The section of the Rio Grande below Lajitas is the most popular with boaters. Just downstream from the small town, the river enters Big Bend National Park on the Texas side. Initially the river winds its way past a series of hills composed of a mix of igneous and sedimentary rocks. As the river approaches Santa Elena Canyon, it flows through several minor rapids. The igneous rocks so dominant in Colorado Canyon are soon left behind; an igneous sill intruding into layers of Boquillas limestone in the cliffs of Mesa de Anguila is one of the last traces of igneous material near the river for many miles. Unlike Colorado Canyon, the rest of the Rio Grande's canyons are cut through sedimentary rock, chiefly limestone.

Because it is inaccessible by road,

The downstream mouth of Santa Elena Canyon is one of the most famous landmarks in Texas

Rafts regularly float Santa Elena Canyon

29

few people visit the river between Lajitas and the downstream mouth of Santa Elena Canyon, except by boat. The Rio San Carlos flows into the Rio Grande just above the canyon. The permanent stream originates in mountains to the south in Mexico. Along the way it passes through the old Spanish colonial town of San Carlos. Boaters often stop at the confluence to wade up the small, narrow side canyon cut by the creek. Its water is generally much clearer than that of the muddy Rio Grande.

A quarter mile downstream from the Rio San Carlos confluence, the river enters the short, but impressive, Santa

Elena Canyon. The gorge is the most famous canyon in the Big Bend country, cutting a winding path through a huge limestone fault block. The fault block creates a large mesa that tilts upward, climbing gradually from the southwest to northeast and terminating abruptly in a series of high cliffs at the Terlingua Fault

on the northeast side. The river created the canyon by eroding its way through the mesa. Because of the strong, homogenous nature of the limestone, the river cut a very deep and narrow canyon rather than a broad valley. Several geologic formations are exposed in the canyon walls, but the Santa Elena and Del Carmen limestones of the Cretaceous Period form most of the dramatic cliffs.

The upstream entrance is impressive, with the river flowing abruptly into a sheer-walled canyon about two hundred feet deep. The mesa on the Texas side of the river is known as the Mesa de Anguila; the mesa on the Mexican side is called the Sierra Ponce. As the river winds deeper into the canyon, the walls rise, eventually reaching 1500 vertical feet above the river at the downstream mouth of the canyon. The limestone layers, tilting upward toward the northeast, create the optical illusion that the river is falling faster than it really is.

One of the most exciting rapids along the Rio Grande in the Big Bend country lies in the heart of the canyon. Thousands of years ago a section of the sheer canyon wall weakened and collapsed into the river. The huge rubble pile probably temporarily dammed the river until the water's erosive power cut its way through. Today the river still winds its way through a tricky maze of giant boulders. Strong currents, eddies, sharp bends, and rapids make the Rockslide a serious hazard to boaters. The portage around the Rockslide is difficult, but usually necessary for canoes and inexperienced boaters.

The narrow slot of Fern Canyon enters the river downstream from the Rockslide. The canyon is so narrow that the sun strikes the canyon bottom only briefly

Fern Canyon

The Rockslide presents a serious obstacle to boats

31

The Rio Grande enters a broad valley below Santa Elena Canyon

each day. A small spring-fed stream sometimes cascades down the polished rock of the canyon, providing water to several groups of ferns.

The Rio Grande flows from the canyon with an even more dramatic exit than its earlier entrance. As the river crosses the Terlingua Fault, the canyon walls abruptly fall away. The river enters a valley with broad floodplains and turns in a more southeasterly direction.

Terlingua Creek flows into the river at the mouth from the Texas side, usually adding a small flow of clear water.

The next ten miles of river floodplain, plus the area upstream along Terlingua Creek to Terlingua Abaja, were once farmed intensively to supply food to the miners in Terlingua. Later, cotton and wheat were grown on the fertile flats using river water. Once the land on the Texas side became part of Big Bend

National Park, the farms were abandoned. Adobe ruins mark the sites of the old farmhouses on the gravel hills above the floodplain.

Across the river sprawls the small Mexican village of Santa Elena. The residents make their living by ranching, farming on the Mexican side of the floodplain, and catering to the visits of tourists. The villagers run a small ferry boat across the river.

The remnants of Castolon sit on a low mesa across the river from Santa Elena; the historic buildings house a store, ranger station, and museum. In the past, the buildings served as residences, a post office, and a trading post. Although park visitors probably account for most of the store's business, it is an important shopping place for the residents of Santa Elena. It is a long and difficult drive for them to reach any other significant towns.

Below Castolon and Santa Elena, the river winds through forty miles of broad floodplain and low hills with great looping bends. Some of the loops curve so sharply that the river flows west for a distance and the view north looks into Mexico. Only a few minor rapids stir up the river between Castolon and Talley. About 25 miles downstream from Castolon, the river passes a ford probably used by the Comanches on the eastern fork of the their great war trail. In several spots the rough River Road of Big Bend National Park and its short spurs touch the river. A few ranches and farms once lay along the Texas side of the river, but only ruins remain. Here and there an isolated farm or ranch still exists on the Mexican side. Finally, at the old Talley ranch site, the river enters Mariscal Mountain and cuts another of the major canyons of the Rio Grande.

MARISCAL CANYON

Mariscal Canyon is the narrowest canyon in the Big Bend, and in some ways the most spectacular, although only about six miles long. From a distance, the upstream canyon mouth appears as a crack in Mariscal Mountain. Since the mountain slopes steeply, the canyon walls become very high only a short distance into the narrow gorge. The cliffs rise almost 1500 feet straight up from the river. Above the canyon, the Rio Grande begins to flow east rather

Rafts in Mariscal Canyon

33

Mariscal Canyon

Tight Squeeze rapid

than southeast. As the river enters Mariscal Canyon, it decisively swings northeast, creating the turning point, or big bend, of the Rio Grande for which the entire region is named.

Just inside the canyon entrance, the river flows through the Rockpile, a tricky, but smaller and less hazardous version of the Rockslide in Santa Elena Canyon. Less than a mile further downstream, an immense boulder has fallen into the river creating the Tight Squeeze, the most difficult rapid in Mariscal Canyon.

Halfway through the gorge, the walls

The Rio Grande cut a deep, narrow gorge through Mariscal Mountain

retreat where two side canyons enter from both sides. A faint old smuggler's trail climbs up Cross Canyon on the Texas side and over Mariscal Mountain to the old Solis farm site downstream from Mariscal Canyon.

After the break in the canyon created by the two side canyons, the river enters the second part of the gorge, only to exit in about two miles. The river passes the ruins of the Solis farm on the Texas side before entering the small but scenic San Vicente Canyon. The river carved the canyon through the north end of the Sierra San Vicente, an anticline similar to Mariscal Mountain.

Below San Vicente Canyon, the Rio Grande winds through open country for another ten miles. Along the way it passes several abandoned farms and ranches on the Texas side and the Mexican village of San Vicente, site of the old Spanish presidio. Only adobe rubble remains from the old fort.

Below San Vicente, several hot springs flow from the banks of the river. As the Rio Grande enters Hot Springs Canyon,

Sand dune near Rio Grande Village

Tornillo Creek adds a small amount of water from the Texas side. Although the creek is small and unimpressive at the confluence, it drains much of the eastern side of Big Bend National Park. Like Terlingua Creek, it used to be a much larger flowing stream, lined with cottonwoods and inhabited by beaver. Extreme overgrazing and its by-products—soil erosion and a lowered water table—greatly changed its character, perhaps forever.

Several large hot springs flow into the river just downstream from the Tornillo Creek confluence. J.O. Langford homesteaded here in 1909 and developed a small health spa using the spring waters. Border unrest caused by the Mexican revolution forced the Langfords to leave for several years, but they returned to build motel rooms, a general store, and a post office. They finally left in 1942 after selling their land to the federal government for the national park. Maggy Smith operated the resort for several more years as a park concession before it finally closed for good. The Park Service has preserved several of the buildings because of their historic value. Hot water still bubbles up into the old bathhouse foundation on the river bank, attracting thousands of visitors every year.

Below Hot Springs Canyon, the Rio Grande flows past broad flatlands on the Texas side that were farmed in the early 1900s. Today Rio Grande Village occupies the site, providing visitor services such as campgrounds, a store, and a visitor center. A large spring that forms a jungle-like swamp on the east side of Rio Grande Village harbors the Big Bend mosquitofish, *Gambusia gaigei,* found nowhere else in the world.

The ferry crossing to Boquillas,

The sun sets on the Sierra del Carmen and Hot Springs Canyon

Palm trees mark the remains of Langford's health spa

Mexico lies just downstream from Rio Grande Village. Many visitors to Big Bend National Park ride the small ferry boat across the river to the town. The village was originally settled by workers from the mines in the Sierra del Carmen, the towering mountains just east of Boquillas. Several large hot springs on the Mexican side flow into the river near the town. Downstream from Boquillas, the river flows past the old crossing point of the aerial tramway used by the mines. Just beyond the tramway, the river flows into the heart of the Sierra del Carmen, entering the last major canyon that lies within Big Bend National Park.

37

Moon over Boquillas
Canyon walls

*Desert vegetation clings to
boulders in a side canyon*

Boquillas Canyon

BOQUILLAS CANYON

The Sierra del Carmen rises like a wall on the east side of Big Bend National Park, creating a seemingly impenetrable obstacle for the Rio Grande. The Sierra del Carmen is the largest range in the region, dwarfing even the Chisos Mountains. The long chain of northwest-southeast-trending mountains starts north of Big Bend National Park near Alpine, where the mountains are known as the Del Norte Mountains. Further southeast, they are called the Santiago Mountains.

South of Dog Canyon in the national park, the mountains are known as the Sierra del Carmen. The sub-range of the Sierra del Carmen between Dog Canyon and the Rio Grande is also known as the Dead Horse Mountains. One story of the name's origin tells of a Texas Ranger captain killing some horses belonging to a band of raiders near the mouth of Boquillas Canyon. Another tells of a local rancher's favorite saddle horse being killed when it fell from a cliff in the mountains. The mountains, which slowly rise to the southeast, are notoriously dry, with few springs or other sources of surface water. Chihuahuan Desert vegetation cloaks the range.

Boquillas Canyon splits the Dead Horse section of the Sierra del Carmen from the main range in Mexico. Although the walls rise about 1500 feet from the river, the canyon is not quite as narrow, nor do the walls rise quite as abruptly, as in Mariscal and Santa Elena canyons. However, its length of 17 miles makes Boquillas considerably longer than the other two canyons.

Church at La Linda, Mexico

Boquillas is the easiest Big Bend canyon to float

South of Boquillas Canyon, the Sierra del Carmen rises rapidly in elevation. A large fault created the massive limestone escarpment that towers a vertical mile above the village of Boquillas, Mexico. At sunset, the last rays of the sun turn the white limestone cliffs shades of pink, red, and purple, perhaps giving rise to the their name. Sierra del Carmen means Pink, or Rose, Mountains in English. The dramatic increase in elevation of the mountains attracts additional rainfall. Behind the escarpment lie grasslands and scattered pines. Southeast of the high cliffs, the mountains rise to about 9000 feet in elevation. Dense forests of ponderosa pine, Douglas fir, and Arizona cypress cloak the mountains, in stark contrast to the desert along the Rio Grande 7000 feet below. Even scattered patches of aspens thrive among the rocky peaks. The rugged, unpopulated Sierra del Carmen forms the heart of the proposed Mexican protected area.

As the Rio Grande flows through Boquillas Canyon, it passes a number of dry side canyons on both sides of the river. One canyon, directly across the river from a rock pinnacle known as Rabbit Ears, cuts a deep, narrow slot, little wider in some places than an arms-span.

The river flows quietly through Boquillas Canyon, with only a few minor rapids. The Rio Grande flows out of the canyon as abruptly as it entered, leaving the high cliffs of the Sierra del Carmen behind.

Below the canyon, the river winds through broad open country and around several small islands. About four miles below the canyon's mouth, the river leaves Big Bend National Park. The land on the Texas side is part of the privately owned Adams Ranch. The wild and scenic rivers legislation gives the National Park Service jurisdiction over the river and floodplain below the high water mark. Just past the ranch, Arroyo del Veinte enters the Rio Grande on the Mexican side, creating the only significant rapid on this stretch of river. Soon after the rapid, the river flows under a one-lane bridge, the first road crossing of the river since Presidio, almost 200 miles upstream. The bridge serves the Mexican village of La Linda. Until 1990, fluorite mines in the Sierra del Carmen and a processing plant provided the basis of La Linda's economy. The mine owners used the private bridge to haul the product north to the railroad in Marathon. The plant is now closed, and its future status is uncertain. Below the bridge, canyon walls begin to rise again, leading into the final series of Rio Grande canyons.

THE LOWER CANYONS

Some of the wildest country in Texas lies along the 140 miles of river between La Linda and Langtry. Once the bridge is left behind, few signs of people are encountered other than occasional fishing camps and abandoned dwellings. Most of the river's first twenty-five miles below the bridge flow past the Black Gap Wildlife Management Area on the Texas side; the rest of the land on the Texas side is privately owned.

The river passes through a series of canyons during its trip to Langtry; most have several names and so are lumped

The Lower Canyons

41

together under the name Lower Canyons. Below the bridge, the Rio Grande quickly enters the first canyon, sometimes referred to as Temple Canyon. Thick beds of Cretaceous limestone wall in the river, similar to the three main canyons in Big Bend National Park. Eight miles further on, the river flows out of Temple Canyon into a broad area known as Outlaw Flats. The dry Maravillas Creek, a major drainage that stretches all the way to Marathon, enters the river. For the next ten miles, the river flows tranquilly through a broad valley. East of the river a notable butte, Cerro el Barco, dominates the valley on the Mexican side.

A few miles past Cerro el Barco, the canyon walls again start to creep closer to the river. Just past the eastern boundary of Black Gap Wildlife Management Area, Big Canyon and Reagan Canyon join the river from the Texas side, creating the first rapids of the Lower Canyons. Since its bend at Mariscal Canyon, the Rio Grande has been trending northeast. After Reagan Canyon, the river begins its turn east and then southeast toward the Gulf of Mexico.

The confluence of Reagan Canyon marks the start of the most spectacular section of the Lower Canyons. The valley walls close in rapidly, trapping the river in a narrow corridor. For the next 43 miles the cliffs rise straight from the river bottom, pinching the floodplain into narrow strips of green that come and go. The walls tower as much as 1500 feet above the Rio Grande; the adjacent uplands rise more than 2000 feet above the river. The river is wild and almost inaccessible from above.

The Rio Grande winds its way through the narrow gorge, passing caves

hollowed out of the high cliffs and deep side canyons. Many years ago, rancher Asa Jones built a series of pumps and pipelines on the canyon wall to water his ranch above the canyon rim on the Texas side. He also operated a large candelilla wax extraction operation on the ledge at the top of the first cliff. The remains of his projects still cling to the cliffs.

Below Asa Jones' water works, the large San Rosendo Canyon joins the Rio Grande, creating Hot Springs Rapid, the first major rapid of the Lower Canyons. A large, popular hot spring on the Mexican side gives the rapid its name. Several adobe houses, sometimes occupied by Mexican goatherders, rest on a bench above the spring. Three miles downstream from Hot Springs Rapid, the Rio Grande cuts through the Bullis Gap Range. The range was created by a large anticline, or fold in the earth's crust, known as the Bullis Fold.

San Rosendo Canyon

The Rio Grande above the confluence with Big Canyon

The river cuts through thick beds of steeply dipping Santa Elena limestone.

The debris dumped into the river by two more side canyons creates two moderate rapids in the next ten miles of river. The first Berlandier ash trees appear, indicating the gradually changing climate and vegetation as the river loses elevation and moves closer to the Gulf of Mexico.

The river makes a sharp bend around the 1000-foot tall promontory of Burro Bluff and roars through the largest rapid in the Big Bend country, Upper Madison Falls. Many rafters and almost all canoeists portage the rapid created by the mass of boulders and debris washed in by Mexico's Arroyo del Tule. Two miles down river, a rockslide creates another more moderate rapid, Lower Madison Falls. Several thermal springs issue from the Texas bank below the rapid.

A few miles below Lower Madison Falls, the Rio Grande tumbles through a moderate rapid where Panther Canyon joins the river. The canyon walls start to lower gradually, although they are still spectacular.

A massive gorge, San Francisco Canyon, joins the river from the Texas side where the cliffs have fallen to about 600 feet in height. The normally dry side canyon drains a vast area and periodically causes catastrophic flooding of the Rio Grande. The book *River Guide to the Rio Grande: The Lower Canyons*, published by the Big Bend Natural History Association, tells of the flood on November 5, 1978. After heavy rains fell on the watershed, water roared out of San Francisco Canyon, reaching a depth of forty feet at the confluence. Downstream, the Rio Grande rose to 55 feet, largely because of the San Francisco Canyon floodwaters. The rushing water scoured the river floodplain leaving little vegetation.

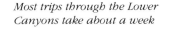

Most trips through the Lower Canyons take about a week

The canyon walls are low near Dryden Crossing

About two miles below San Francisco Canyon, the high walls begin to recede and the river winds through low hills in a shallow canyon to Dryden Crossing, the most popular take-out point for float trips through the Lower Canyons. Along the way, Sanderson Canyon joins the river. Although it appears unimpressive at the river, the canyon drains a large area and is also notorious for floods. Dams now control its flooding.

In the next 55 miles between Dryden Crossing and Langtry, the Rio Grande flows languidly through a landscape of low hills and bluffs. Only one short canyon, the scenic El Indio Canyon, lies along the route. During normal lake levels, the river flows into Lake Amistad a few miles above Langtry. The last of the Rio Grande's wild character ends.

The Pecos River flows into the lake

downstream from Langtry. The National Park Service manages Amistad National Recreation Area for boating, camping, fishing, and general recreation. Seminole Canyon, a side canyon entering the lake, contains many large, well-preserved pictographs dating back thousands of years. The caves holding the ancient rock art are protected in Seminole Canyon State Historical Park.

Below Lake Amistad, the river winds its way across hundreds of miles of mesquite studded plains, its waters slowly depleted by cities and agriculture. In its fertile lower valley and delta, the river irrigates thousands of acres of farmland. Finally, polluted and depleted and not even a stone's throw wide, the once-mighty Rio Grande dumps the last of its waters into the Gulf of Mexico at Boca Chica.

Pictographs at Seminole Canyon

45

VISITING THE RIO GRANDE

Although the Rio Grande travels through 340 miles of mostly wild and undeveloped country as it flows from Presidio to Langtry, it is accessible in many places. Texas highway FM 170 parallels the river between Presidio and Lajitas. The river is easily accessible in Big Bend National Park at Castolon, Santa Elena Canyon, Hot Springs, and the Rio Grande Village/ Boquillas area. High clearance and four-wheel-drive vehicles can reach isolated parts of the river along the rough River Road. Between the head of Boquillas Canyon and Langtry, the river is only easily accessible by vehicle in one place, the La Linda bridge. All other access points, such as Dryden Crossing, require permission from private landowners or a permit from the Texas Parks and Wildlife Department to enter Black Gap Wildlife Management Area.

To truly appreciate the river, you need to get out of your car and walk a bit. Drive to Santa Elena Canyon early in the morning and stroll down to the river bank, through a dense thicket of willow, mesquite, huisache, and tamarisk. As the sun rises, the towering walls of the canyon entrance turn a pale pink and then a rich gold before brightening into full daylight. Follow the trail across Terlingua Creek and into the canyon, up over the cactus-covered ledges of Glen Rose limestone, and into the thickets of cane that line the narrow floodplain. On cool mornings, the melodic descending song of the canyon wren echoes from the cliffs. The brown, muddy river water hisses by, almost silently. The first morning breeze rustles the tall stalks of cane. Soon other visitors arrive, breaking the spell of solitude along the river.

Another easy hiking trail accesses the mouth of Boquillas Canyon. A nature trail beginning at the Rio Grande Village campground provides a tremendous view of the river and the towering limestone escarpment of the Sierra del Carmen. One of the most popular trails in Big Bend National Park leads along the riverbank under a shaly cliff to the old bathhouse of Langford Hot Springs.

Mariscal Canyon and Boquillas Canyon can be viewed from above by hiking the Mariscal Canyon Rim Trail and Marufo Vega Trail, respectively. Only experienced hikers should attempt these hikes; the trails are strenuous, hard to follow, and brutally hot in summer. The rim of Santa Elena Canyon can be

The Sierra Ponce near Santa Elena

reached by following the faint maze of trails scattered across Mesa de Anguila. Mesa de Anguila hikes should be attempted only by fit backpackers who are skilled at reading topographic maps.

In Big Bend Ranch State Natural Area, highway FM 170 provides easy approaches to the river in several places. Although trails have not yet been developed along the river in the new state park, it's easy to walk along the banks at the access points used by boaters.

Although hikes along the Rio Grande are rewarding, nothing quite equals floating the canyons of the Big Bend. In October, 1899, Dr. Robert Hill was the first person known to successfully float the Rio Grande from Presidio to Langtry. Many others had tried before, but all had met failure, if not disaster. Today, with better equipment and knowledge, thousands of people float sections of the Rio Grande every year.

Boquillas Canyon has the smallest

rapids and is the easiest trip of the major canyons, especially for less experienced boaters. Boquillas Canyon trips generally take two to three days. Boquillas and Mariscal canyons are the only major canyons within the National Park Service's jurisdiction that it recommends for open canoes.

Upstream from the national park, Colorado Canyon has several small rapids but provides one of the best canoe trips in Texas. Colorado is the most easily accessible canyon of all; some segments can be run in less than a day.

The Rockslide in Santa Elena Canyon creates a serious hazard for any type of boat, but especially for open canoes. Over the years, quite a few boats have been lost in the boulders and swift currents of the rapid. The Rockslide can be portaged, but not without great difficulty. With rafts and experienced boaters, the rapid can usually be negotiated with little trouble. The spectacular gorge, combined with easy put-in and take-out points, make the one or two day Santa Elena trip the most popular in the Big Bend.

Because of the rough roads to the put-in and take-out sites, Mariscal Canyon is the least floated in the national park. The Tight Squeeze and Rockpile are tricky, but not as hazardous as the Rockslide in Santa Elena Canyon. Mariscal is a short canyon, but particularly impressive with its very narrow gorge.

Sooner or later, the true Big Bend river rat will float the Lower Canyons from La Linda to Dryden Crossing. Because the trip usually requires six to seven days, a very long shuttle, and passage through several major rapids, it's probably the least traveled section of

Kayak in the Lower Canyons

Giant dagger yuccas

river. However, the Lower Canyons lie in true Texas wilderness. Boaters float for days through spectacular canyons and encounter no roads, no power lines, no bridges, and very few other signs of humans.

To float the canyons in Big Bend National Park or the Lower Canyons, a permit must be obtained from the rangers at Big Bend National Park. Alternatively, boaters may self-register at the Stillwell's store for Lower Canyons trips. Permits for Colorado and Santa Elena Canyons can be obtained at the Big Bend Ranch State Natural Area headquarters in Lajitas. Novices and newcomers should consider taking a commercial trip with one of the outfitters in Study Butte, Terlingua, and Lajitas. Otherwise, start with an easy day trip, such as Hot Springs Canyon, and then follow with a longer, more difficult trip such as Boquillas Canyon. People contemplating boating the Rio Grande should talk to a ranger at Big Bend National Park. Several guidebooks describe in depth the necessities for a river trip.

Boaters on the Rio Grande can relax and enjoy the lazy pace of the river, punctuated occasionally by the thunder of a rapid. The sheer canyon walls slide slowly past beneath the deep blue Big Bend sky. High above, vultures circle effortlessly, buoyed by rising thermals. An occasional splash marks a catfish sliding through the water below. Prickly pear cacti, ocotillo, and lechuguilla cling to almost impossible ledges. The Rio Grande, one of the longest rivers in North America, embraces life in the Big Bend country, beautiful and serene.

Canoe near Boquillas

Inside Back Cover: Big Bend bluebonnets with margined perityle

Back cover: Mariscal Canyon